ISBN #: 978-1-365-70753-7
Content ID: 20505733
Book Title: Beach Drunk

"The sound of rain needs no translation.."

- Zen Master

Contents

Introduction

Beach Drunk

Drunk and happy swinging
in the breeze laughing
        to the sound of the ocean
as the water calmly walks
        to the shoreline & suddenly
                crash tackles the cliff
and the birds caw for blood
as the spotlight moon patrols the skies.
Beach Drunk, swinging and swaying to the
        rhythm of the sea
watches the clouds play with the moon.
While Mr Insomniac cries into his sodden sheets
        wishing time would speed up
        or stop
        stop already
and he curses the names of all the tasty
        poisons that led him this far.
As Beach Drunk, singing an old sea shanty about
        love & loss & betrayal, leans over a rail
        searching for oblivion in sea and waves
but instead vomits the last lumps of his
        sick stomach into the sea.
While Mr Insomniac sticks his head in an oven
        and They find him.
        Hot. Cooked. Cold.
        but at peace   at rest

and the cops suspect foul play
        except for the note left by
        Mr Insomniac:
"suffering is fixed easy
        by suicide
eternal sleep was better than none;
        not drinking sent me mad!
And and and! AND!
        peace *was* necessary;
I regret nothing except for
        giving up the drink:
and I'm sorry I can't write more
        God is stalking me!"

Beach Drunk walks off the beach
                happy knowing
that in the time it takes to walk there
the bottle-o will be open.

Books

gloomy April day—
I'll be 27 soon,
oh, look! a bookshop

in the insomniac's
morning, another novel
flung at the wall

beatific ramblings—
        Ginsberg's collected
makes a good pillow

Coffee

god in the coffee
art—takeaway lid
seals in the heat

Charlie Parker in
the café—I've been reading
Kerouac again

engrossing tattoos—
a café wallflower too
embarrassed to write

through ran-speckled
        glasses
the barista's smile

coffee cups spill from
office bins—traffic limps home
dusty & beaten

our morning coffee
run—close enough to touch, too
distant to notice

Beach

whiskey memories—
        I sit in the surf,
no bottle this time

waves slap
the rocks—coffee stains
on a notebook

        hot summer's day
children play along the beach—
a mum looks frantic

fish swim around my
ankles—a seagull circles
in a cloudless sky

hands clasped—
waves
lap the shore

sweep of fisherman's net—
    school of fish
    refract sunlight

pillowed by the dunes—
stargazing with
a pint of whiskey

beachside bonfire—we
dance in circles, no one cares
about tomorrow

sunburnt neck—
trail of sand from front
door to bathroom

her green eyes—
he’s washed
his surfboard 3 times

no sign of winter—
sunscreen bottles used to prop
up books in the sand

sunset—
we dance on
a seashell mosaic

A la Kerouac

that girl's beautiful
but she wasn't at the tutorial
—I died!

ethereal beauty—
I've only
seen your words

not for the
faint-hearted—
an empty bed

blue shirt
black blouse—
    no tea left!

whiskey doldrums—
    bottle-o's still
closed!

    frost
on the lawn—
kettle boils

her pale blue eyes
in winter seaside sunrise
road trip beginnings

arm-in-arm we are
a tobacco haze wafting
through tourist-stuffed streets

her tattoo sleeve...wait!
...would it be called
tattoo legging?

someone suggested
gym...is my 3 hours nightly
writing not enough

faith in religion—
caterpillar unable
to metamorphose

Renga

1.

that one song which sends
you away from everything;
its melody moves

you viscerally to a
better mental space. A place

which helps you to keep
perspective, stay grounded, &
remember your self;

it's that one lyric which has
become prayer for mindfulness

2.

After visiting The Museum of Medieval Stockholm

we look over Lake
Mälaren having a smoke
before entering

museum built on remains
of medieval Stockholm—

for such a tiny
country, the Swedes kicked arse in
the Baltic Region;

nice of them to have all the
descriptions in English though

3.

"be present" they say;
my mind only presented
me with the Void that

makes up my current future—
"Look UP" they cry, as though

anxiety &
depression have dimensions
which follow logic

of a healthy mind—when really;
I am my open fists

4.

we've wasted too
many good ideas on
vacuous businesses

who don't understand it's
simply to improve profits—

offered up too much
of our creativity
only for it to

be jettisoned into the
digital Void, a stillbirth

5.

her smile as she jumps
on him coming off the plane—
I step around their

moment juggling luggage &
phone for directions to a

taxi, ignoring
tender scenes all around me—
scenes of families,

friends, lovers glad their loved ones
returned amongst us tourists;

a happy buzz of
people reuniting—I
desperately needed

rest; peace; to forget why I
had travelled solo again;

but these tender scenes
encircling me, reminded
me of that lyric;

"You can travel on 10,000
miles and still stay where you are"

Interlude

Beer

Christ with Lucifer sipping
        beer and talking
shop
Lucifer is a bored
     man, a tired
          jaded
fallen angel in need
        of a break.
He wants to make
   a certain soul
his stand-in while
   he goes for the old
holidays
   with his
wife & kids.

Loud Visions

Five whiskeys and a beer later

the club is an altogether different place –

with throbbing floor and pulsating furniture,

pleasurably insidious bass pumping;

bodies move instinctively

to the beat.

Sweaty, writhing, wriggling bodies rub up against

one another – flailing to the infectious

beat, push and bounce to the bass mouthing lyrics

half remembered.

Sweaty, writhing wriggling bodies pulse and shake

as the music consumes the crowd and creates a desire to be

close, caressing the nearest person non-sexually sexually.

Getting lost listless and careless in a sea of writhing,

wriggling bodies meshing together in a sweat bath of the

dark closed-in claustrophobic strobe-lit club crushing together

in a crescendoing pulsing dance.

Untitled

I'll toast this glass
to the god of drunken
writing & the next glass
will toast Dionysus
after that
I'll toast any god
who smiles kindly
on creation
through destruction

Accent

her lilting accent gives
English renewed beauty,
becomes a filter of uncertainty
bashfulness lending
an innocence to the language—
when we part ways,
with her number in my phone,
I throw my poetry
notebook in the bin

& go home to freshen up.

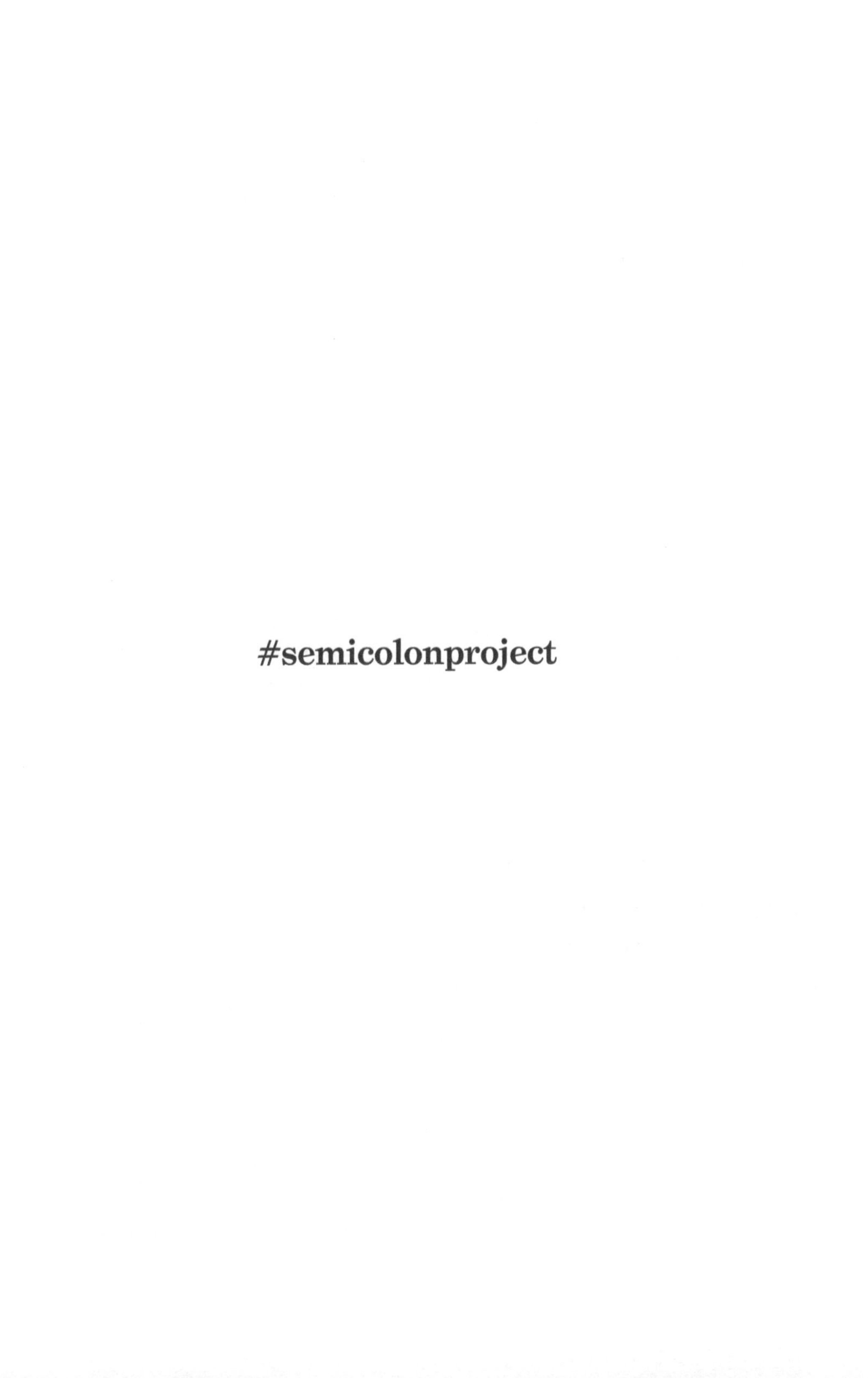

#semicolonproject

not all stories
are told in ink—
scar tissue wrists

prayer beads pass
between distracted fingers—
late night train delay

fingers caress faint
traces of history on
moon light pale forearm

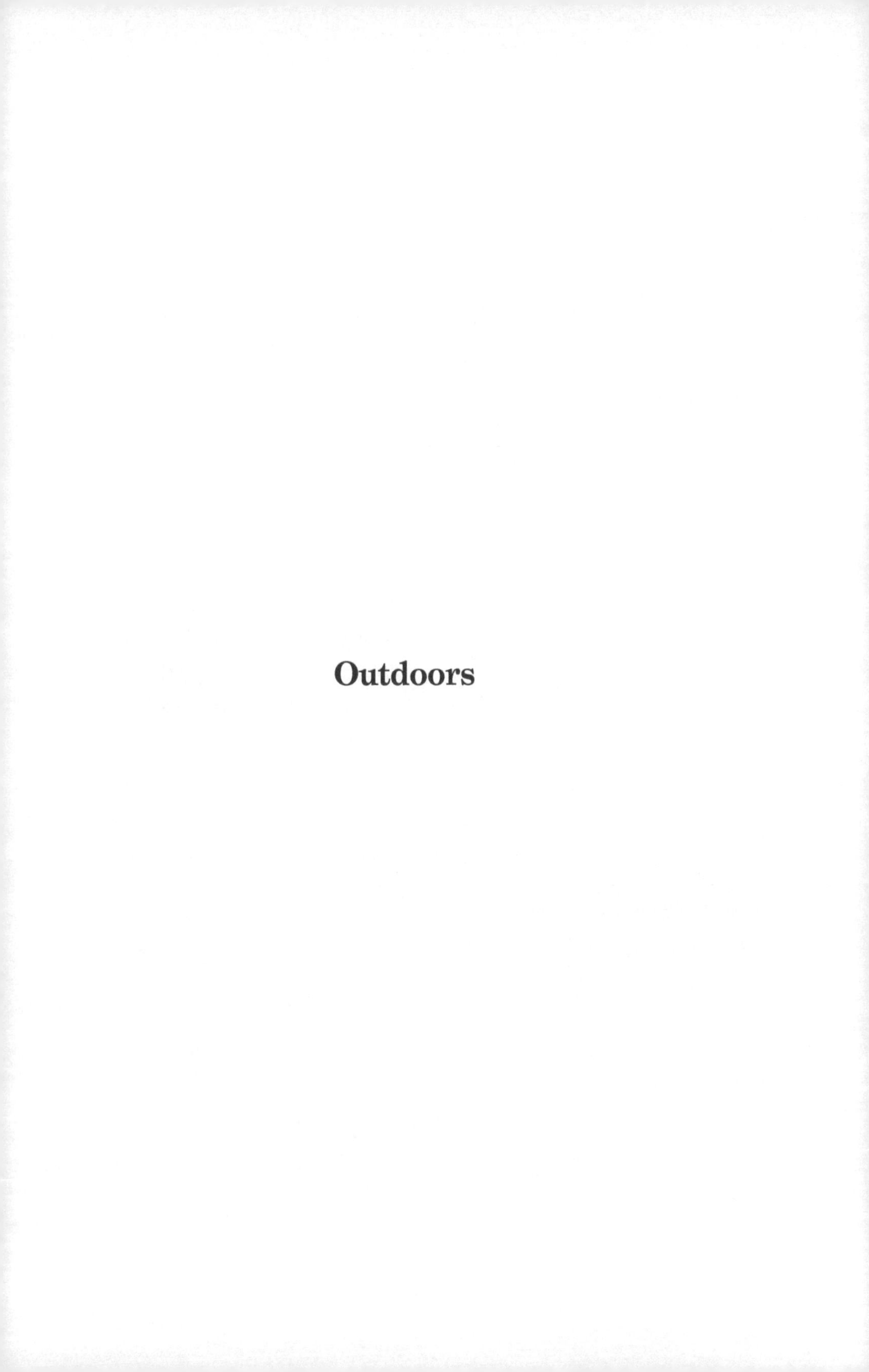

Outdoors

twig snaps—
        birds burst
from the trees

early morning walk—
alcohol & cheap perfume
pervade the sidewalk

rose petals float
downstream—her feet
over the bridge

wood smoke—
potatoes wrapped
in tin foil

cloud of breath—
marshmallows
over a fire

radio
turned up—feet
on the dashboard

seated in the shade,
    a stray cat stares
at her next meal

first drops
of rain—car
door closes

leaf
on the page—
afternoon sun

queueing for
        a theme park—
god, I love Summer

the Aussie Summer—
a theology of surf,
BBQs and drink

congested traffic—
Kerouac's weird jazz-style record
plays on the iPod

sun through
the trees—no, wait!
it's raining

busking with frost
on the bow—flower tilts its
head in search of sun

pebbles skip across
the water's surface—fish &
chips in newspaper

frangipanis bloom—
dog paddles out
to get his stick

hobo tunelessly
sings a Kristofferson song—
food thrown to seagulls

cloudless midday sky—
even the kookaburras
are too hot to sing

Night In

rain lashes
the beach—
wine & movies

gin drips from
the table—bodies
coiled on the couch

burnt offerings—
someone call
for pizza

stars in her eyes—
drinking chess
on a cloudless night

wine by the fire—
rain
on a tin roof

Night Out

tasting a memory—
        snogging
in the nightclub

congealed blood—
broken bottles
sparkle in the dawn

sifting through
        flavours—
foggy taste of last night

faint trace
    of regret—
lipstick stains

halogen-lit
    love story—
not enough vodka

bass-heavy music—
warmth of alcohol
    & flesh

vomit drips from
the bin—taxis prowl
outside the clubs

a brief glimpse across
the room—how easily it
is to fall in love

buying her
        a drink—a
poem for tomorrow

ANZAC Day

wheelchair veteran—
　　a bugle sounds
at the break of day

Afterword

Possibility

He's eyeing his pint warily.
His girlfriend sits down reluctantly
        and takes a pull from a Corona.
A brief look between boredom and distaste
passes over her face as she looks her
boyfriend over.
Sluggishly the boyfriend's hand flies out
to catch the pint angrily;
        he gulps his beer with
claw-like hands that grip the glass as he hunches his
        shoulders and neck into the drink.
Slurred, violent sounding speech slops out in fragments
        and his girlfriend stares sullenly through him –
A faint glint is in her eye of her own possible happiness.
Surveying the room she smiles at the drummer
        as he smiles at her over the rim of his drum.
She glances over once or twice again
        that far away glint growing a little brighter and
        her smile growing a litter bigger.
Until an obtrusive voice, thick with drink,
        cuts to her brain shutting down
        the spark.
When the Drummer looks up again
all he sees is an empty glass.

www.ingramcontent.com/pod-product-compliance
Ingram Content Group UK Ltd.
Pitfield, Milton Keynes, MK11 3LW, UK
UKHW041914190726
13854UKWH00003B/1241